JUV
E
964
V2
T73
2003
TOMAN

D1247040

CHICAGO PUBLIC LIBRARY
TOMAN BRANCH
4700 S. PULASKI
CHICAGO, IL 60623

THE HISPANIC INFLUENCE IN THE UNITED STATES

LATIN?S

IN AMERICAN HISTORY

MARIANO GUADALUPE

VALLEJO

BY KATHLEEN TRACY

Mitchell Lane

PUBLISHERS

P.O. Box 619
Bear, Delaware 19701

THE HISPANIC INFLUENCE IN THE UNITED STATES

LATINOS

IN AMERICAN HISTORY

OTHER TITLES IN THE SERIES

Visit us on the web: www.mitchelllane.com
Comments? email us: mitchelllane@mitchelllane.com

R04009725O2

THE HISPANIC INFLUENCE IN THE UNITED STATES

LATINOS
IN AMERICAN HISTORY

MARIANO GUADALUPE
VALLEJO

BY KATHLEEN TRACY

Copyright © 2003 by Mitchell Lane Publishers, Inc. All rights reserved. No part of this book may be reproduced without written permission from the publisher. Printed and bound in the United States of America.

Printing   1   2   3   4   5   6   7   8   9

Library of Congress Cataloging-in-Publication Data
Tracy, Kathleen
    Mariano Guadalupe Vallejo/Kathleen Tracy
        p. cm. — (Latinos in American history)
    Includes bibliographical references (p.) and index.
    Summary: Profiles the man called one of California's most important founding fathers, who fought for the rights of the Native Americans there while paving the way for California to join the United States.
        ISBN 1-58415-152-8 (lib bdg.)
        1. Vallejo, Mariano Guadalupe, 1808-1890—Juvenile literature. 2. Military governors—California—Biography—Juvenile literature. 3. Mexican—California—Biography—Juvenile literature. 4. Pioneers—California—Biography—Juvenile literature. 5. Frontier and pioneer life—California—Juvenile literature. 6. California—History—To 1846—Juvenile literature. 7. California—History—1846-1850—Juvenile literature. 8. California—Biography—Juvenile literature. [1. Vallejo, Mariano Guadalupe, 1808-1890. 2. Pioneers. 3. Mexicans—California—Biography. 4. California—History—To 1846. 5. California—History—1846-1850.] I. Title. II. Series.
F864.V2 T73 2002
979.4'04'092—dc21
[B]   2002066067

ABOUT THE AUTHOR: Kathleen Tracy has been a journalist for over twenty years. Her writing has been featured in magazines including The Toronto Star's "Star Week," *A&E Biography* magazine, *KidScreen* and *TV Times*. She is also the author of numerous biographies including "The Boy Who Would Be King" (Dutton), "Jerry Seinfeld - The Entire Domain" (Carol Publishing), "Don Imus - America's Cowboy" (Carroll & Graf), "Lorenzo De Zavala," and "William Hewlett: Pioneer of the Computer Age," both for Mitchell Lane. She recently completed "God's Will?" for Sourcebooks.

PHOTO CREDITS: Cover: Northwind Picture Archives; p. 6 Bancroft Library/University of California; p. 9 Danny Lehman/Corbis; p. 10 Bettmann/Corbis; pp. 12, 14, 15, 17 Northwind Picture Archives; p. 18 Richard Cummins/Corbis; p. 21 David G. Houser/Corbis; p. 24 Northwind Picture Archives; p. 26 Corbis; p. 28 Robert Holmes/Corbis; p. 29 Archive Photos; p. 30 Bettmann/Corbis; p. 32 Northwind Picture Archives; p. 34 Corbis; p. 36 Northwind Picture Archives; p. 38 Bancroft Library/University of California; p. 40 Lowell Georgia/Corbis; p. 42 Bettmann/Corbis

PUBLISHER'S NOTE: This story is based on the author's extensive research, which he/she believes to be accurate. Some parts of the text might have been created by the author based on his/her research to illustrate what might have happened years ago, and is solely an aid to readability for young adults.

The spelling of the names in this book follow the generally accepted usage of modern day. The spelling of Spanish names in English has evolved over time with no consistency. Many names have been anglicized and no longer use the accent marks or any Spanish grammar. Others have retained the Spanish grammar. Hence, we refer to Hernando de Soto as "de Soto," but Francisco Vásquez de Coronado as "Coronado." There are other variances as well. Some sources might spell Vásquez as Vazquez. For the most part, we have adapted the more widely recognized spellings.

CONTENTS

CHAPTER 1

CHAPTER 2

CHAPTER 3

CHAPTER 4

CHAPTER 5

CHAPTER 6

This view of San Francisco was created by M. F. Swasey around 1884. It depicts Yerba Buena, renamed San Francisco in 1847, as a small, sparsely populated town before the discovery of gold in the nearby Sierra Nevada Mountain Range.

VIVA MEXICO!

In the early morning hours of September 16, 1810, a 57-year-old Catholic priest named Miguel Hidalgo y Costilla stood in front of the people of the small town of Delores. The town was in New Spain, the vast North American area colonized by the Spanish that included modern-day Mexico and the California, New Mexico, and Texas territories.

After three hundred years of Spanish rule, the same desire for freedom that inspired the American colonists to break away from England during the War of Independence in 1776 had begun to fuel a similar revolt in New Spain. The criollos, or people of Spanish descent who had been born in Spanish America, were tired of not having the same rights and privileges as the gachopines, native Spaniards living in Mexico. Their goal was to establish Mexico as an independent country within the Spanish empire.

Hidalgo's sympathies, however, were not necessarily with the criollos. The well-educated priest had long sought to improve the lives of the native Indians who in many cases were treated as slaves. Even though it was against gachopine law, he taught them how to plant various crops, and he built an estate where the people of the community could learn carpentry, tanning, and pottery.

So Hidalgo was already considered a troublemaker when he joined forces with other liberal-thinking activists who were opposed to being under Spanish rule and who wanted the freedom to govern themselves. Hidalgo and his compatriots, or partners, agreed to start a revolution in October 1810.

However, word of the pending criollos revolt was leaked to the gachopine authorities. They put out an order to arrest Hidalgo and other criollos, which is what prompted the priest to make the most important decision of his life: Rather than be taken prisoner, he decided to start the uprising immediately. But he rejected the idea of letting the area remain within the Spanish empire. Instead he believed Mexico should be completely free. Spain, and all the gachopines, were the enemy.

When Hidalgo rang the church bell to call the local Indians to church, instead of saying mass and preaching his usual sermon that morning, he stood up and announced it was time for Mexico to be a truly independent country. In an impassioned speech, he urged the Mexican townspeople to reclaim the land stolen from their ancestors and to drive out the Spaniards who had treated them so badly. *"Mexicanos,"* he shouted to the crowd. *"Viva México!"*

And with that rallying cry, the Mexican revolution began. Hidalgo formed a band of soldiers made up of local Indians and marched toward Mexico City, engaging in a series of victorious battles along the way. He traveled from town to town, inciting the people to take up arms and fight for their country.

The following year Hidalgo was ambushed and captured. After being stripped of his duties as a priest, he, along with several other members of the original group of revolutionaries, was executed. Spanish officials hoped their deaths would put an end to the rebellion, but it didn't. Others followed in Hidalgo's footsteps, and the war for Mexican independence dragged on for over 11 long and horribly bloody years. Finally Spain admitted defeat.

After the war, California officially became a Mexican territory, but the Spanish influence on the land remained strong. Because California was located at the northern frontier of New Spain, few of the people living in the region experienced any of the horrors of the war. And at first, living under Mexican rule didn't seem much different than what life had been like under Spanish rule.

Alta California, the area north of Baja, or Lower, California, was first discovered by Europeans in 1542 by Juan Rodríguez Cabrillo. The area was claimed by Spain in 1769 after Gaspar de Portolá established a settlement on San Diego Bay and later in Monterey, which was named the capital of Alta California.

Then in 1776, Juan Bautista de Anza founded Yerba Buena, where he built a presidio, or military fort, further increasing Spain's foothold in the

Father Hidalgo, depicted in this painting, was considered a troublemaker when he wanted Mexico to be an independent country, free from Spanish rule. During the Mexican Revolution, he was executed.

This is an illustration of Father Junipero Serra in his priestly dress. Serra was a Spanish missionary called the "Apostle of California." He founded numerous missions in California while he looked out for the rights of the Native Americans.

New World. Yerba Buena would later become known as San Francisco once California came under American rule.

In order to more efficiently colonize Alta California as a Spanish territory, Spain's King Carlos III ordered three types of settlements to be established: Franciscan missions, presidios, and small villages called pueblos, which would grow food for the soldiers at the presidios. Among those who volunteered to come to Alta California to help settle the land was a Franciscan missionary named Father Junípero Serra, who was traveling with Portolá and who immediately established a mission at San Diego. His goal was to convert as many of the local Indians as possible to the Catholic religion, and in so doing make them loyal to Spain.

One of the places where he built a mission was Sonoma. Centuries before Spanish explorers would claim the land for their country, the ruggedly beautiful coast and fertile valley of the Sonoma area were home to the indigenous Pomo and Miwok Indians. These Native Americans lived peacefully, and their way of life had remained unchanged for countless generations. But the arrival of the missionaries abruptly altered everything. Within just a few years, the Sonoma Indians would see their land taken away, their culture nearly erased, and their people treated as slaves, forced to help build and maintain the missions. Although the missions were integral in settling Alta California in general and Sonoma specifically, turning it into an important agricultural center, the treatment of the Native Americans during that time is considered a sad chapter in the area's history.

But to the missionaries, the end goal of spreading their faith justified the means they took to do so. So up and down the coast of Alta California, from San Diego to San Francisco, Father Serra continued to build missions, using local Indian labor to turn the surrounding land into productive farms and cattle pastures. The presidios provided protection from pirates, and nearby pueblos began to grow into towns as the population of colonists increased. These colonists were called Californios, Spanish and Mexican settlers who had been born in Alta California, and their way of life was closely tied to the fertile land.

Because they lived so far away from where the central Spanish, then later Mexican, government was located, their culture developed with little or no interference from authorities. However, as American settlers from the East Coast began arriving in greater numbers in the mid-1800s, there were some Californios who began to envision a new way of life. These people helped pave the way for California to become part of the United States.

One such visionary was Mariano Guadalupe Vallejo (Vuh-YAY-hoe or Vuh-LAY-oh). Like Father Hidalgo, Vallejo would fight for the rights of the Native Americans and would see his homeland embroiled in a war for independence. But unlike Hidalgo, Vallejo's accomplishments have been overlooked through the years, despite his being called by many one of California's most important founding fathers.■

THE CALIFORNIA COAST
UNDER THE MEXICAN RÉGIME.

SCALE OF ENGLISH MILES.

100   200

This is a map of California when it was under Mexican rule. You can locate many of the places mentioned in the story on this map.

THE CALIFORNIOS

B y the turn of the 19th century, the population of Alta California was a diverse mix of native Indians, Spanish settlers, and Californios. Mariano Vallejo's grandparents, who had immigrated to the New World from Bilbao, Spain, were among the many pioneer families to put down stakes and colonize the region. As a reward for their efforts, some of the European settlers were given land by the Spanish, which most used to raise cattle.

The thirst for adventure that compelled the Vallejos to leave Spain in favor of an untamed land was passed on to Ignacio, Mariano's father. In 1775, when he was 26 years old, he decided to quit his religious training and do some exploring of his own. He joined the Mexican army as a leather-jacket soldier. These soldiers, who were stationed at presidios, wore sleeveless jackets made of deerskin, horse-hide, or cowhide, which protected them from Indian arrows. A year later Ignacio was one of the soldiers who accompanied Father Serra to San Francisco to establish a mission there. During his time in the military, Ignacio Vallejo would

This portrait of Mariano Guadalupe Vallejo was drawn from a photograph by Bradley and Rulofson. It is one of the few images of him that survives today.

serve at seven of the missions founded by the priest and would rise to the rank of sergeant.

In 1791, Ignacio married 13-year-old Maria Antonio Lugo. They eventually settled in Monterey, the provincial capital of Alta California, where Ignacio worked as an engineer on irrigation projects. He was successful and lived a prosperous lifestyle, thanks to the large land grants he had been awarded by Spain as compensation for helping protect the missions as a soldier. He and Maria lived in a large, well-furnished adobe home adorned with red tiles. Adobe houses were popular because they were very comfortable—cool in the summer and warm in the winter.

Like many well-to-do Californios, Ignacio and Maria had a large family, with 13 children. Their eighth child, Mariano Guadalupe Vallejo, was believed to be born July 7, 1808, although historical records disagree, with birthdates of July 4, 1807, and July 5, 1807, also given. What is known for sure is that he grew up with eight sisters and four brothers in his parents' home.

The settlers who lived in Spanish California were required to learn a variety of trades and then teach them to their servants. Like all young men at the time, Mariano was taught from a young age many skills, such as learning how to ride horses; how to make goods such as soap, pottery, and candles; and how to tan hides.

Along with the other local Californio boys, Mariano attended the mission school and was considered a diligent student. But like his father, Mariano had an inquisitive mind, and he wanted to learn more than just the lives of the saints and religion. He soon got his wish.

In November 1818, a French-born pirate from Argentina named Hippolyte de Bouchard attacked the presidio at Monterey with a 40-gun warship, forcing the Spanish defenders inland. Governor Pablo Vincente de Sola sent the local women, children, and livestock away to the safety of the San Antonio and Soledad missions. Mariano and most of his siblings left Monterey with their mother, while Ignacio and his eldest son stayed behind to defend the city. However, they were no match for the pirates' firepower. Bouchard and his men ransacked the city, then set it on fire.

As a result, when he was 11, Mariano went to study with Governor Sola, who was a friend of Ignacio's. Sola taught the youth social and practical skills, such as etiquette and accounting. Mariano, who up to that time

This is a rendering of Maria Antonia Lugo, General Vallejo's mother.

spoke only Spanish, learned English, French, and Latin. Meanwhile, Sola expressed his personal political views to Mariano, who would come to share many of the same beliefs as an adult.

Although Mariano did not realize it, he was being carefully groomed for a life of public service. He had been two years old when Miguel Hidalgo started the war for independence, and he was 13 when Mexico finally achieved its freedom from Spain in 1821. Amazingly, because communication was so slow, Californios did not learn the war was over until a year after it ended. While the war had dragged on, though, it seemed clear to many what the outcome would eventually be. Both Sola and Ignacio Vallejo realized that the young nation would need leaders and believed Mariano had the intelligence and abilities to be one of them. For his part, Mariano looked forward to Mexican self-rule with great anticipation. He believed local governments should represent the people's interest, and he envisioned an end to political corruption; he hoped to promote both. However, he would do so without his longtime mentor and teacher.

Pablo Sola would be the last Spanish governor of Alta California. After news of Mexican independence finally reach him, Sola said goodbye to the Vallejo family and returned to Mexico City in 1822. Mariano was then appointed the personal secretary to Sola's successor, Luis Arguello. Two years later, in January 1824, when he was still just 15, Mariano joined the Mexican army as a cadet. As Sola and Ignacio Vallejo had anticipated, Mariano proved to be a natural-born leader, and in 1827 he became a member of the territorial legislature. He also quickly rose through the military ranks: By the time he was just 21, Vallejo was in charge of 150 men.

In 1828, an expedition under Vallejo's command successfully defended the San José mission against an uprising instigated by an Indian named Estanislao. Estanislao had run away from the mission and later returned with a band of warriors. Vallejo diffused the situation and eventually Estanislao returned to the mission. His handling of the potentially serious revolt merely added to his already impressive reputation and led to his being appointed commander of the presidio at San Francisco.

In 1833, Jose Figueroa became the new governor. He had great respect for Vallejo, and the two became close and trusting friends.

Despite all his responsibilities, life wasn't all work for Vallejo. Mariano had also found the time to fall in love. In 1832 he married Francisca Benicia Carrillo, the daughter of one of the first woman winemakers in Sonoma County. As a young bride, she traveled by mule for four weeks while pregnant to reach her husband in Sonoma. Although neither of them knew it, the timing for starting a family couldn't have been better, because Vallejo would soon become one of the wealthiest landowners in all of Alta California.■

Francisca Benicia Carrillo, the wife of Mariano Vallejo

Mission San Francisco de Solano remains today in the Sonoma State Historic Park. This was the last mission built in Alta California and the only one constructed after Mexico's independence.

CHAPTER 3

SONOMA

Although Alta California was part of a newly independent nation, life there didn't seem that much different under Mexican rule than it had under Spanish rule. However, one change was significant. When Father Serra and the other Franciscans had established the missions, the settlements were supposed to have been temporary. Once the native people had been converted to Christianity and the friars had finished acculturation, the missionaries would supposedly leave and the mission lands would be distributed among the neophytes, the Indians who had converted to Christianity. This process of distributing the mission lands to local people was known as secularization.

However, none of that ever happened under Spanish rule. For almost 60 years, the missionaries controlled all the mission lands, and it seemed unlikely they would ever give it up willingly. So after Mexican independence in 1821, Californios and others began to call for secularization. Part of the desire to break up the missions was political. The Mexican constitution promoted equality among all Mexicans, regardless of race, and many people believed the missions were unconstitutional. The missions had discriminated against the Native Americans by forcing them to work and not giving them the same rights as the Europeans who settled the area. Likewise, the Native Americans had begun to rebel against missionary control, and revolts were becoming more common.

More than anything, though, the native-born Californios saw the missions as standing in the way of economic progress and individual prosperity, because by controlling so much of the best agricultural and grazing land, it prevented individuals from establishing successful ranches and farms.

In 1834, Governor Figueroa finally issued a proclamation ordering the secularization of the California missions. The breakup of the mission had an immediate and dramatic impact on the Alta California social structure. Almost overnight, a new upper class of Californios was created. This small group consisted of families who had been given ranchos, or huge cattle ranches. The land guaranteed those families wealth and power in the community.

These land grants came with *diseños,* or maps, so that the new owners would know where the boundaries of their ranchos were. The maximum size for a private rancho land grant was supposed to be about 50,000 acres, but this limit was often ignored, and some people received multiple grants.

Around the time Governor Figueroa secularized the missions, he also gave Vallejo a new promotion, appointing him military commander and director of colonization of the northern frontier. With the new title came a new assignment: In addition to controlling any Indian uprisings, Mariano had to go back north and take charge of the mission

San Francisco de Solano in the Sonoma Valley. It was the last mission built in Alta California and the only one constructed after Mexico's independence.

Vallejo's duties included turning the mission into a parish church, freeing the Indian workers, and distributing the mission lands among the local population. He was also instructed to help colonize the area. Russian expeditions had come down from Alaska to participate in the lucrative sea otter trade and had established several outposts, including Bodega Bay and Fort Ross. The governor didn't want the Russians getting any ideas about claiming the land as their own, so the goal was to crowd out the Russians by increasing Spanish colonization. Typically, though, Vallejo got along well with the Russians he met, which may have prevented any disputes over land from occurring.

This is a photograph of the restored mansion of Mariano Vallejo in Sonoma, California.

As a reward for the work he had already done and for the large assignment he was being given, Vallejo was granted 44,000 acres in the Petaluma Valley to develop as a private rancho. According to local historical records, it was an area Vallejo referred to as "a land of enchantment." Mariano had already earned military success and political respect. The property guaranteed him wealth, setting the stage for him to become one of the most influential men in California—all while he was still in his 20s.

Once in Sonoma, Vallejo set out both to follow his orders and to make a home for himself and his family. While he began building a house, to be called La Casa Grande, on the Sonoma plaza, Vallejo also laid out the plans for the pueblo he was to establish. This would become the first town to be planned and settled in the territory north of San Francisco under Mexican rule. He gave it the Indian name of the valley, Sonoma, which means "Valley of the Moon."

The next part was getting people to move there. He encouraged both Mexican and American settlers to come to Sonoma, and even sold them parts of his land at excellent rates as incentive. To protect the new community, Vallejo brought his troops from the San Francisco presidio to Sonoma. He also organized a company of about 50 Indians and taught them how to shoot weapons so that they could help defend the pueblo as well. When the Mexican government failed to pay the troops, Vallejo himself footed the bill for their clothes and food. During his first few years in the area, Mariano and his troops actually lived in the mission. He used the soldiers to help build the town, which included plazas, parade grounds, vineyards, a fort, and Vallejo's large mansion.

In addition to his work in Sonoma, Vallejo laid the foundation for establishing a local government at San Francisco. On January 1, 1835, he turned over the control of all civil matters to San Francisco's *ayuntamiento*, or town council.

His more liberal political beliefs were evident in the way he disbursed the mission land. Although under Spanish rule the Indians had been turned into second-class citizens with no voting rights, Vallejo sought to make some amends. He granted Suisun Indian Chief Solano a large tract of land.

The alliance between the chief and Vallejo helped them both. On one hand it helped keep Indian revolts in the area to a minimum, while on the other it allowed the region to maintain a large population of Native Americans.

Like most historical figures, Vallejo was a man of his time. And during that time Indians were not considered equal. While Vallejo was instrumental in improving their standard of living, he still held on to some of the old Spanish ways. For example, although he was supposed to distribute mission property to the Native Americans, he claimed much of the land as his own. Instead of giving them their own plots, he offered local Indians protection, room, and board in exchange for their labor. As a result, on Petaluma Rancho, he was able to oversee 10,000 head of cattle, 4,000 horses and 6,000 sheep, making it one of the largest ranchos in the state.

Perhaps more importantly, though, is that Vallejo was seen, by both the settlers and the Indians, as a fair and just man. That said, he was also known to have a quick temper and was especially upset by behavior he considered defiant or disrespectful, no doubt an outgrowth of his military train-ing.

By 1837, Lieutenant Vallejo was one of the richest and most powerful men in Alta California. Under his leadership, Sonoma flourished and there was peace. His adobe home on the plaza at Sonoma, La Casa Grande, attracted visitors from around the world. It was one of the largest and most nicely furnished private homes in California. Along with his wife and children—who would eventually number 16, including two who were adopted—Vallejo was living a dream life.

But within a few short years, everything Mariano had built would be suddenly and stunningly taken away from him.■

This adobe house was built by General Vallejo around 1834.

WINDS OF CHANGE

In 1835, Governor Figueroa died. In October of that year, José Castro was appointed to take his place. However, his tenure was short: In January 1836, the Mexican government appointed Nicolas Gutiérrez to succeed him. The new governor was greatly disliked, in part because he was Mexican and not Californio, and in part because he was considered a bad leader who didn't put the interests of the people first. Opposition quickly grew against Gutiérrez, and he stepped down from office in May. However, he was replaced by an equally disliked official named Mariano Chico, who upset the people even more by insisting on a centralized government that would take local decisions out of the hands of the citizens.

When Chico left in July to get help from Mexico to quell the budding rebellion, Gutiérrez returned as acting governor. Chico never returned. Later in 1836, one of Vallejo's nephews, Juan Bautista Alvarado, and former governor José Castro led a rebellion against Gutiérrez. One of Alvarado's

Bird's-eye view of Monterey, California, overlooking the town and busy harbor.

promises to the people who supported him was that he would name his uncle Mariano Vallejo as his second in command.

Alvarado led a small grassroots army to Monterey and forced Governor Gutiérrez and other top Mexican officials to surrender. They ordered the officials to leave California and return to Mexico. Alvarado then declared California to be a "free and sovereign state" within the Mexican Republic, meaning it would have total control over its internal affairs. In 1837 a compromise was reached wherein Mexico agreed not to interfere with the state and California would remain part of the Mexican Republic. Alvarado was officially named the governor of California.

Although there is no indication that Vallejo actively participated in the uprising, he also did nothing to stop it. That's because despite his high rank in the military and the wealth he had accumulated since Mexico's independence, Vallejo was critical of the Mexican government and in fact

believed California would be better off being part of the
United States. Not only did Vallejo believe in democracy,
but from a practical standpoint, he believed the United
States would better stabilize the area economically and
socially.

After Alvarado was installed as governor, he named his
uncle commandant general of all Mexican military forces in
California. And for the next five years Californios ran the
territory without any interference from Mexico. During that
time, under Vallejo's guidance, Sonoma grew and diversified.

While California was under Spanish rule, trade had been
restricted and only Spanish or Mexican ships were allowed
into harbors along the coast. After Mexican independence,
the new government welcomed trade from all countries.
Another change was that foreign nationals were welcome. In
fact, Vallejo used many foreign carpenters while building
Sonoma. Many of the sailors and workmen ended up marry-
ing local women and settling permanently in the area.

It was necessary to get official permission to immigrate,
and Mexico strictly enforced its laws against illegal immigra-
tion. However, California needed skilled men, so immigra-
tion was granted if the petitioner agreed to become a Mexican citizen and join the Catholic Church. But California was
also being transformed by the number of people traveling to
the territory in search of goods and plentiful hunting.

The first Americans to arrive in California included
Jedediah Strong Smith and a group of other fur trappers,
They came in 1826 by way of a new trail they had discov-
ered that wound through Utah, Arizona, and the Mojave
Desert. When they showed up unexpectedly at the San
Gabriel mission, the trappers were looked on with suspicion,
and Smith was placed under house arrest. They agreed to
leave and returned home, this time via a different trail. Al-

though their visit was cut short, the trails traveled by Smith and his companions soon became common knowledge, and the number of Americans and other immigrants migrating to California rapidly increased.

Among those who arrived in California was John Sutter. He had been born in Germany but came to America to escape huge debts he had amassed in Europe. In 1839 he arrived in California and received permission to establish his own permanent settlement, which he called New Helvetia, east of San Francisco along the Sacramento River. He was granted 50,000 acres in exchange for promising to protect the area from intruders, such as rebellious Indians or trappers.

He built Sutter's Fort near present-day Sacramento. Within a few years, he had 13,000 cattle and a thriving crop of grain. The fort became a common rest stop for Americans coming into California, and Sutter became a wealthy and influential man.

In 1841 the Russians decided to abandon their outposts at Bodega and Fort Ross. That same year the first wagon train of overland settlers from the United States arrived in

Sutter's Fort in Sacramento, California

California. These pioneers, who in the eyes of Mexican law were illegal immigrants, often had skills that the Californios lacked—such as business management and administration, bookkeeping, and accounting. Vallejo welcomed them, in part for their skills and in part because he believed it was inevitable that the United States would eventually take over California, for the good of the region and its people.

The reforms and improvements Vallejo had hoped for under Alvarado's rule had not materialized. His disappointment prompted him to write a letter to the authorities in Mexico, explaining that because of his unhappiness with Alvarado and his belief that California's potential was being destroyed, he wanted to be relieved of his command. He also noted that the offices of governor and commandant general be joined into one position.

Mexico responded by naming Manuel Micheltorena governor and commandant general. When Micheltorena arrived in Alta California, Vallejo gave food to his army, which was made up of *cholos*, or former convicts paid to be soldiers, and loaned him several thousand dollars. In return for his generosity, Micheltorena granted

John Augustus Sutter (1803-1880) built New Heveltia at Sutter's Fort. On January 1848, while building a sawmill, James W. Marshall found gold on Sutter's land. In the Gold Rush of 1849, his workmen deserted him, his cattle were stolen, and his land was overrun with squatters, causing him to declare bankruptcy in 1852.

Mariano the 80,000-acre Rancho Nacional Soscol, further increasing Vallejo's massive land holdings, which now totaled more than 175,000 acres.

Micheltorena proved to be no more popular than Gutiérrez or Chico had been. The reason was simple: Californios felt they had little in common with Mexico and resented its authority over them. The local pride felt by Californios in both the northern and southern parts of the state further dissolved the perceived bond between California and Mexico. In the end, the people who made up Alta California—Indians, Californios, and an ever-growing population of American pioneers—saw themselves as Californians, not Mexicans.

Moreover, Micheltorena's army of *cholos* committed terrible acts against the populace during their march to Monterey, infuriating Californians everywhere. The inevitable revolt against Micheltorena occurred in 1844, this time from a group made up of both Northern and Southern Cali-

Governor Juan Bautista Alvarado (left) (1836-1842) and Governor Manuel Micheltorena (right) (1842-1845)

fornians. Although people from the upper and lower region of the territory tended to be rivals and looked at each other with suspicion, they were united in their desire to oust the governor.

Throughout the conflict Vallejo had once again refused to take sides, but his actions made his position clear. Although he would not actively take up arms against the sitting governor, he disbanded his own Sonoma forces in 1844 and informed the governor he could no longer financially support them as he had been doing.

The uprising was short-lived. Micheltorena successfully beat back the northern army led by José Castro, near San José, but he was defeated in Los Angeles by 400 Californios led by Juan Bautista Alvarado at the bloodless Battle of Cahuenga in February 1845.

Nobody was killed in the skirmish, and after both sides ran out of ammunition, Micheltorena withdrew. He agreed that he and his army would leave California. Reasserting their north-south rivalry, after Micheltorena was ousted, Pio Pico was made the civil governor at Los Angeles, with José Castro setting up a rival regime in Monterey.

No doubt Micheltorena and his superiors realized that for all practical purposes, Mexico's control over Alta California was over. It would soon become official.■

Mexican troops moved through the American Southwest before the Treaty of Guadalupe Hidalgo in 1848, where Mexico ceded almost 50 percent of its territory to the United States.

BEAR FLAG REVOLT

CHAPTER 5

During the 1830s and '40s, the people of America were on the move. Spurred by a healthy economy and the pioneer spirit, many families headed west, lured by the promise of wide-open spaces and the chance to build a new life. Although many Americans thought of the West as desolate, areas such as Texas and California were already populated by indigenous Indians, as well as by Mexican and Spanish settlers. Their way of life would abruptly change as the United States set out to fulfill its Manifest Destiny—the belief that it was the country's right to claim all of North America in order to further its economy, cultural traditions, and political beliefs.

The relationship between the Americans and Californians was friendly until late 1845, when a U.S. soldier named John C. Frémont arrived in the area with a force of 60 men. Officially in California on a mapmaking expedition, Frémont would wind up the central figure in one of the more confusing episodes in California history. Historians cannot agree whether Frémont was a loose cannon, a fanati-

In early 1846, John C. Frémont rode to Gavilan Peak and raised an American flag, vowing to fight to the last man to defend it.

cal military man, or just a mischief maker. But whatever his motives, he managed to turn settlers and Californios—who up until then had lived in peace—against one another.

In early 1846, Frémont received permission from governor/commandant José Castro to camp for the winter in an area by the Colorado River. Instead, he and his men headed west toward the populated areas of the Santa Clara Valley and Monterey. When he learned that Frémont was not where he was supposed to be, Castro sent a messenger to tell him he must leave the area at once. Frémont rode to Gavilan Peak and raised an American flag, vowing to fight to the last man to defend it. Castro gathered an army and prepared for a battle, but after a few days Frémont left, apparently headed north to Oregon.

After Frémont left, rumors began circulating among the settlers that because of the standoff with Frémont, Governor Castro was going to order all the Anglos out of California.

Tensions between the Californios and immigrant settlers mounted quickly. When Frémont returned, he easily persuaded a group of American settlers to stage a revolt. They overpowered some of Castro's soldiers and took their horses, which had just come from Vallejo's Sonoma rancho.

On June 14, 1846, another group of settlers, on orders from Frémont, stormed the presidio in Sonoma, then surrounded General Vallejo's home. His wife, Francisca Benicia, begged Mariano to escape, but he refused, worried his family might get hurt. Instead, he agreed to give up his land and his mansion and be taken prisoner in exchange for his family's safety.

In hindsight it seems illogical that Frémont would arrest Vallejo, who openly supported California's becoming part of America. Many historians believe Frémont was motivated not by political ideals but by simple jealousy—he resented Vallejo's respect, power, and wealth.

After Vallejo was taken to Sutter's Fort, where he was to be held prisoner, William B. Ide was chosen commander in chief and proclaimed the creation of the Bear Flag Republic. William Todd, the nephew of future president Abraham Lincoln, created a flag for the new Republic using a three-by-five-foot piece of muslin cloth. In the upper left-hand corner, he painted a five-pointed red star, and in the center he drew a California grizzly bear. Along the bottom edge was strip of red flannel, and written across it were the words *California Republic.*

On July 5, Frémont forced Ide to sign a proclamation making Frémont the commander in chief of the Bear Flag Republic and its military. He assumed command of the renegade settlers, and along with his own men called his new army the California Battalion.

What nobody knew was that the United States was already at war with Mexico, intent on acquiring the huge area

William Todd created a flag for the new Republic using a 3 X 5-foot piece of muslin cloth. In the upper left-hand corner, he painted a five-pointed red star, and in the center he drew a California grizzly bear. Along the bottom edge was a strip of red flannel, and written across it were the words California Republic.

of land that was under Mexican rule, from the western border of Texas through Northern California. Some Americans, including President James K. Polk, who was a Southerner, wanted to take the land from Mexico in order to promote slavery. Others simply believed it was Manifest Destiny. Either way, American troops moved in to claim the land.

On July 7, 1846, the U.S. Navy captured Monterey, and Commodore John D. Sloat claimed California for the United States. Two days later they reached Sonoma. Navy Lieutenant Joseph W. Revere, grandson of Paul Revere, lowered the Bear Flag and replaced it with the American Flag. The Republic instigated by Frémont had lasted less than a month. In the end the military action set in motion by Frémont had been pointless, and the only lasting effect was bitterness between Anglo-Americans and the Spanish-speaking Californios.

Meanwhile, back at Sutter's Fort, Vallejo remained imprisoned. Sutter, a longtime friend of Vallejo's, had been shocked when Frémont arrived with Mariano as his prisoner and ordered he be treated as such. After Frémont left, Sutter made sure Vallejo and his associates had comfortable rooms and plenty of good food to eat and were allowed out several times a day. Even so, Vallejo's health suffered, and he was no doubt emotionally devastated to be treated as an enemy when he had promoted union with America for so long.

In August, U.S. Commodore Robert F. Stockton ordered Vallejo freed and allowed him to return home. Or to what was left of it. Vallejo was sickened to discover that his rancho had been thoroughly looted by the Bear Flaggers. All his horses and livestock were gone, as were many of his personal belongings. After so many years of service to California, Vallejo was faced with the daunting task of starting over.

According to *The Beginnings of San Francisco* by Zoeth Skinner Eldredge, in September 1846, Vallejo wrote to his friend Thomas O. Larkin, "The political change has cost a great deal to my person and mind and likewise to my property. I have lost more than one thousand live horned cattle, six hundred tame horses, and many other things of value which were taken from my house here and at Petaluma. . . . All is lost and the only hope for making it up is to work again."

The war with Mexico lasted another year and a half. While the Californios in the north aided the U.S. soldiers, those in the south resisted. Although General Stephen W. Kearny defeated the southern Californios in 1847, the fighting continued for another year in Mexico, until the U.S. Army invaded Mexico City.

Mexico signed the Treaty of Guadalupe Hidalgo in 1848 and formally ceded almost 50 percent of its territory to the United States. Today this area is called the American Southwest. Vallejo had lived to see his vision for California come true, but at a cost he had never imagined. And Vallejo's sacrifices weren't over. ■

This is a view of Sutter's Mill, California where James Wilson Marshall struck gold in January 1848, accidently starting the California gold rush. Since communication was slow in those days, it took almost a year for word to spread around. The official announcement of the discovery was made in December 1848 during President Polk's farewell address.

THE GOLD RUSH

A week before the Treaty of Guadalupe Hidalgo was signed, a carpenter named James Wilson Marshall was building a sawmill for John Sutter at the American River. On the morning of January 24, he was checking the mill's tail-race when he spotted something in the water. It was gold.

When Marshall told Sutter what he had found, Sutter swore everyone to secrecy. But word quickly leaked out, and soon the California Gold Rush was on. The state would be forever changed.

The first published accounts of the discovery of gold at Sutter's Mill appeared in San Francisco's two weekly news-papers in March 1848. In the beginning few people took notice—until an entrepreneur named Sam Brannan saw an opportunity. First, he stocked his store at Sutter's Fort with goods and merchandise he thought gold seekers would need. Then, on May 12, 1848, Brannan went to San Francisco, pulled out a bottle of gold dust, and ran through the streets. "Gold!" he shouted. "Gold from the American River!" This time, people paid attention.

However, the official announcement of the discovery wasn't made until December 5, 1848, during President Polk's farewell address. It was then that the gold rush began in earnest, which is why the flood of prospectors who came to California were called "forty-niners" instead of "forty-eighters."

During 1849 it is estimated that around 80,000 people came to California. By today's populations that might not seem like a lot, but consider that in 1846, just three years before, fewer than 1,000 Americans were living in California with its approximately 12,000 Californios. Within a few months San Francisco's population swelled from under 500 to over 20,000 people. In all, $10 million worth of gold was mined in 1849, and over the next ten years, $550 million would be taken from the earth.

In a bitter twist of fate, the gold rush proved to be the ruin of John Sutter. First, all of his workers quit to go mine for gold. Then squatters, people who use

View of California's American River, where gold was accidently discovered in 1848.

property that doesn't belong to them, looted Sutter's land, destroying crops and killing his livestock. By 1852, Sutter was bankrupt and incredibly bitter. He would spend the rest of his life fighting in vain to be compensated for his losses. In 1880, during one of his trips to Washington, D.C., to argue his case, Sutter died.

Despite all the gold that was eventually mined, few people actually struck it rich in the mother lode, as California's rich vein of gold was called. But while many people would go back home, a large percentage of them stayed in California because it offered a variety of opportunities. As a result, by 1852 the non-Indian population of California had soared to over 100,000. With so many people coming to the state, suddenly the land that had seemed so plentiful now seemed in short supply.

In 1848, General Vallejo was one of eight Californios to serve as a delegate to California's constitutional convention, where he advocated giving Indians the right to vote, making slavery illegal in California, and allowing wives to hold separate property—positions that were considered extremely liberal-minded for the time. In 1849 he was elected to the State Senate. In 1850, California became the 31st state admitted to the Union. However, before ratification, or Congressional approval, the lawmakers in Washington, D.C., revoked a provision in the Treaty of Guadalupe Hidalgo that protected the legal rights of Mexicans to maintain their land grants. And with Californios now greatly outnumbered by American settlers, in the end the great rancho owners like Vallejo would be stripped of their land.

Surprisingly, Vallejo did not turn his back on his new country, despite its efforts to take away his land. That same year he offered to donate 150 acres and $370,000 worth of buildings to establish a permanent state capital in a new city he wanted to call Eureka, but which soon came to be known

This lithograph by Kellogs and Comstock shows the mining operations on the western shore of the Sacramento River during the California gold rush.

as Vallejo. In 1852 the city became the first permanent seat of California state government. However, members of the legislature were unhappy with living and working in the rustic town and moved the capital to Sacramento just a few weeks later. For a while, the legislators couldn't make up their minds. Floods forced them back to Vallejo; then they moved to Benicia, a town Vallejo named after his wife, and finally back to Sacramento, which remains the capital to this day.

Even though his dream of having the state capital in the city named after him fell through, Vallejo remained active in local politics. He was elected mayor of Sonoma in 1852 and again in 1860.

Although he remained influential, Vallejo was no longer a wealthy man. In 1855, the U.S. government awarded him only $48,700 of the $117,875 claim he had filed for damages and losses he incurred during the Mexican War. He also spent thousands of dollars fighting to retain his land grants, but in the end most of his land had been taken away. To make ends meet, his wife began selling produce to a local hotel.

In 1866, Vallejo lost his home in Sonoma but was allowed to stay on, paying rent. Most of his income at that point came from owning the water company that supplied Sonoma. Perhaps the cruelest blow came in 1867 when La Casa Grande burned to the ground, destroying Vallejo's five-volume handwritten manuscript, *History of California*.

General Vallejo, as he was still called, spent the last years of his life quietly, reading, visiting with friends, and writing his memoirs at his home, which was located on the last of his landholdings, a two-hundred-acre ranch he called Lachryma Montis, meaning "Tear of the Mountain." On January 18, 1890, Mariano Vallejo died at the age of 82. He is buried in a little cemetery on the hill above Sonoma.

If Vallejo ever regretted his support of California statehood, he never showed it, even though by the time he died it was clear that most Mexicans and Mexican-Americans in California had lost their political power and their wealth and were treated as second-class citizens. To the end, he refused to be embittered, and in his memoirs, he wrote, "The inhabitants of California have no reason to complain of the change of government, for if the rich have lost thousands of horses and cattle, the poor have been bettered in condition." ▪

CHRONOLOGY

1808   born in July (the exact date is disputed), the 8th of 13 children

1818   fled Monterey with mother and siblings after the city was attacked by pirates

1819   was taught English, French, and Latin by William E. P. Hartnell, who went on to found the first junior college in California

1822   was appointed personal secretary to Governor Arguello

1824   entered military service as a cadet at Monterey

1828   defeated Miwok Indians during battle at Indian Mission Estanislao

1832   married Francisca Benicia Carrillo, with whom he would have 14 children and would adopt two others; received property grants for Rancho Petaluma and Rancho Suisun

1833   became military commandant of the San Francisco Presidio

1834   appointed administrator of San Francisco de Solano

1835   named director of colonization in the northern frontier

1836   promoted to commandant general of the "Free State of Alta California"

1841   welcomed first American settlers to California, which was still part of Mexico

1846   arrested and imprisoned by settlers during Bear Flag Revolt

1848   chosen as a delegate to the state constitutional convention

1849   elected state senator, where he promoted Indian rights and lobbied against slavery

1855   awarded $48,700 by U.S. government for damages incurred during the Mexican War

1862   loses most of land after decision by U.S. Supreme Court nullifies his 80,000-acre land grant

1866   loses ownership of Sonoma home; forced to pay rent in order to remain

1867   five-volume handwritten manuscript, *History of California*, is lost when his former home, La Casa Grande, burns to the ground

1890   dies January 18 at Sonoma

TIMELINE IN HISTORY

1542   Spanish explorer Juan Rodríguez Cabrillo comes ashore near modern-day San Diego and declares the land a possession of Spain.

1602   Sebastián Vizcaíno sets sail from Mexico northward and names Cabrillo's bay San Diego after the Spanish Catholic saint San Diego de Alcala.

1769   Gaspar de Portolá establishes a colony on San Diego Bay and California becomes official Spanish colony. "New Spain," as the American territories were called, encompassed an area that included modern-day Mexico, Texas, and California.

1776   Juan Bautista de Anza founds Yerba Buena in Alta California; the settlement will later become San Francisco.

1810   Miguel Hidalgo y Costilla ignites War of Mexican Independence.

1821   Mexico wins independence from Spain.

1834   The California missions are secularized and indigenous Indians are released from slavery.

1836   Juan Bautista Alvarado leads a revolt and declares himself governor of Alta, or Upper, California.

1841   The first American immigrants travel overland to California.

1842   Captain Thomas Jones of the U.S. Navy accidentally seizes Monterey.

1846   Start of Mexican War. In June, John C. Frémont leads Bear Flag Revolt, resulting in arrest and incarceration of Vallejo and his brother Salvador; California is named an independent republic, which lasts only 23 days; Republic of California is declared an American territory in July.

1848   Gold is discovered in Northern California, setting off gold rush; Treaty of Guadalupe Hidalgo is signed and Mexico cedes California to the United States; U.S. Senate repeals Mexican land grants, reducing many formerly wealthy Californio families to near poverty.

1850   California is ratified as the 31st state.

1854   Sacramento is named the state capital.

FOR FURTHER READING

Comstock, Esther. *Vallejo and the Four Flags: A True Story of Early California.* New York: Random House, 1979.

Davis, William. *75 Years in California.* San Francisco: John Howell, 1929.

Dillon, Richard. *Humbugs and Heroes: A Gallery of California Pioneers.* Garden City, N.Y.: Doubleday and Co., 1970.

Empáran, Madie Brown, *The Vallejos of California.* San Francisco: Gleeson Library Associates, University of San Francisco, 1968.

Pitt, Leonard. *The Decline of the Californios.* Los Angeles: University of California, 1969.

Rosenus, Allan. *General M.G. Vallejo and the Advent of the Americans.* Albuquerque: University of New Mexico Press, 1995.

Salonites, Eftimeos. *Berryessa: The Rape of the Mexican Land Grant, Rancho Canada de Capay.* Capay. Calif.: Mission Bell Marketing, 1994.

Sanderlin, George. *The Settlement of California.* New York: Coward, McCann, and Geoghegan, 1979.

Warner, Barbara R. *Men of the California Bear Flag Revolt and Their Heritage.* Spokane, Wash.: Arthur H. Clark, 1996.

ON THE WEB

http://libweb.sonoma.edu/regional/notables/vallejo.htm
http://www.napanet.net/~sshpa/vall.htm
http://www.notfrisco.com/calarchive/governors.html
http://www.pbs.org/weta/thewest/people/s_z/vallejo.htm
http://www.sfmuseum.org/bio/vallejo.html

GLOSSARY

Acculturation (uh-kul-chu-RAY-shun): the process by which people in one culture learn the values, lifestyles and behaviors of people of another culture.

Adobe (uh-DOH-BEE): a building material made of clay and water mixed with straw and horse manure; commonly used to build the California missions.

Alta California: a former Spanish and Mexican province that encompassed today's Northern California.

Californios: the Spanish-speaking Spanish and Mexican settlers who were born in California prior to 1848.

Colonization: the process by which one nation establishes its culture and government in another area of the world, often eclipsing the culture of the indigenous people who lived there first.

Criollo (cree-oh-YO): a person of Spanish descent born in Spanish America.

Franciscans: a Catholic order founded by St. Francis of Assisi in 1209; members established missions in Alta California from 1769 to 1823.

Friar: a member of the Franciscan Order.

Gachopines: native Spaniards living in New Spain.

Indigenous (in-DIJ-ih-NUS): people native to a particular land or area.

Land grants: large tracts of land given to individuals by the government.

Liberal: one who is broad-minded and believes in protecting political and individual freedoms.

Lode: an underground vein bearing gold or other precious metal.

Manifest Destiny: the belief that the westward expansion to the Pacific by the United States was inevitable and necessary.

Mission (MISH-in): church settlement from which friars worked to convert indigenous people to Catholicism.

Mother lode: the main vein of gold or other ore in a region.

Neophyte (nee-oh-FIGHT): a newly baptized mission Indian, or any religious convert.

New Spain: or *Nueva España*, the Spanish empire in the Americas, which was colonized by Spain in 17th and 18th centuries.

Presidio (prih-SID-ee-oh): military forts built in California at San Francisco, Monterey, Santa Barbara, and San Diego by Junípero Serra.

Pueblo (PWEB-low): in Spanish America, the term for "village" or "town."

Rancho: any of the large tracts of land given to Mexican citizens intended for raising cattle.

Secularization (SEK-ye-le-re-ZAY-shun): law passed by the Mexican Congress in 1833 that took the ownership of the missions away from the church and put them into secular, or nonreligious, hands. Missions were turned into parish churches and the lands were divided up among the Native Americans.

Tailrace: The water channel built under a mill for powering the mill's waterwheel.

INDEX